Reading: Revival and Rescue
of Poor Readers

Reading: Revival and Rescue of Poor Readers

by

Peter Coleman, *BA, ACP*
Certificate of Special Education

Hillmead Books

Copyright © Peter Coleman 2006
First published in 2006 by Hillmead Books
1c Hillmead, Norwich, Norfolk, NR3 3PE

Distributed by Gazelle Book Services Limited
Hightown, White Cross Mills, South Rd, Lancaster
England LA1 4XS

British Library Cataloguing in Publication Data
A catalogue record for this book is available from the British Library.

ISBN 0-9552572-0-4
ISBN 978-0-9552572-0-9

Typeset by Amolibros, Milverton, Somerset
This book production has been managed by Amolibros
Printed and bound by Advance Book Printing, Oxford, UK

Dedicated to the many teachers and pupils who have taught me so much.

P.B.C.

About the Author

The author could not read until he was ten years old. He was typical of the many poor readers seen over the ages. He had what he calls dyslexic-type tendencies, whatever name the experts like to call this reluctance to learn to read. Then suddenly, at that age, he discovered a collection of boys' magazines. The pictures were so fascinating that they made him want to know what happened. His parents refused to help him to read 'that trash' when there were plenty of good classics in the house. As is often the case with reluctant readers, he was intelligent enough to use the basic information reluctantly picked up from his patient mother, a teacher. With many tears of frustration he managed to decipher each paragraph of the stories. Thereafter his reading ability improved. Exams were a trial but, finally, he gained a teacher's certificate and a degree from the Open University. Then later, with a specialist course lasting one year, he began the task of lessening the numbers of inadequate readers in secondary schools. It was not long before it became obvious that problems began when the pupils were much younger. If the difficulties could be overcome before the pupils were eight years old then all could be well, as he found.

This book sets out to show this can and has been done. The author's years of personal experience give him more valid authority than many academic masters. He writes in an easy to read non-academic language.

Contents

FOREWORD

Learning to Read

Why do some people not learn to read? It is not lack of intelligence. A person needs some basic abilities such as sufficient maturity of concentration, sight and hearing so that letters can be appreciated, differentiated and remembered. A person needs to realise that when letters are grouped together; making words, that they create clues to the meaning of spoken words, ideas and thoughts. The interpretation of these clues is reading. There are many ways in which these clues may be picked up. Initially a school chooses a particular method, which, it is thought, will prove most understandable to the majority of the children. Some do not understand and therefore fail to learn to read. There may be a number of reasons why a child fails to pick up the clues within the words but most important of all is familiarity with letters. If these are unknown the recognition of words becomes almost impossible; therefore, the recognition of clues as to meaning within words is unlikely.

Although it is not vitally necessary to learn letter names or their order in the alphabet, such knowledge can be very useful. Good readers pick up such information, which disadvantages poorer readers.

When travelling, people often ask directions. Some clues given may be missed or not understood. The traveller asks someone else until, following other clues, the destination is reached. Similarly, in learning to read, if at first directions are not understood, it is necessary to follow other instructions. Some people may be better at explaining and giving clues than others.

The book *Reading: Revival and Rescue of Poor Readers* by Peter Coleman will help and explain what needs to be done to prevent and rescue people who would otherwise become inadequate readers.

INTRODUCTION

When asking any primary school to evaluate the state of reading ability the answer is gratifyingly positive. The school is looking at the picture as a whole. One does not draw attention to the odd ones who have injuries in a football team. Likewise, nobody mentions the few pupils who are a bit behind with their reading. Given time, all will be well. Occasionally the few do not respond as expected. The teachers hope for a 'breakthrough' any day.

This situation is common all over the country in most primary schools. There are many pupils still not reading to the average standard at age nine. Annual reports suggest that twenty per cent are inadequate readers.

Local Education Authorities (LEA) have known this for generations and, periodically, have tried to do something about it. Initially they had payments by results. This meant that pupils were frightened into trying to learn. The general opinion was that either a pupil was lazy or mentally deficient, if he did not learn to read.

Later different methods of teaching were taken up to give an alternative to the old alphabetic approach. Again, most pupils learnt to read but still there were those who did not and ended up as virtual non-readers.

Then, in the 1960s, Reading Clinics were set up. Pupils thought to be intelligent enough were sent for a term. The results were excellent. The average improvement was around two years. This proved that improvement was possible. Then it was found that when pupils returned to their schools, the improvements fell away rapidly. It was concluded that the teaching needed to be school-based.

Then remedial services were begun. Remedial teachers were sent into schools to remedy the deficiencies of pupils' learning. Pupils were over the age of eight years. The idea was to go over the initial teaching again, perhaps on a more personal basis. There was quite a bit of success in some schools but, generally, there were many pupils needing help and too few real experts. As a result a well-qualified teacher was appointed and given assistants. There was no option but to devise a cover-all system of teaching to enable the teachers to do their best for the unfortunate children.

It was found that the success rate was probably no better than if class teachers had assistants. So the Remedial Service, which should have been staffed by experts, fell away, to be replaced by a Special Needs Service.

The idea was that if a school or pupil was in need of special help, a special needs teacher would be sent to help. This is a little nearer to what is actually required. Naturally, parents believe that a special needs teacher is well qualified while the LEA does not disagree. It is not stated how well qualified a special needs teacher should be. Thus the range can be from barely qualified assistant to someone who is able to diagnose the needs of a pupil and supply the appropriate teaching.

The crunch comes when it has to be shown that a pupil has a special need. This takes time so, on average, a pupil does not begin special needs help before the age of eight-plus. Of course, schools do all they can before they apply for a special needs teacher.

The present position appears to be like fighting against a stone wall. 'All is being done that can be done,' is an excuse often heard. If a school found a child of six still not responding to any learning-to-read situations, having a well qualified and knowledgeable special needs teacher on the spot, one might agree, would be the ideal circumstance. In the real world this does not happen. A reception teacher may find as many as twenty-five per cent of her class not ready to learn to read. This is quite normal, for children's intellect grows unevenly and according to previous learning from birth. The reception teacher has to have groups ranging from play groups to ones for those who can read when they arrive at school. The quandary comes when some children are still not ready to learn to read over a year later. Does the teacher struggle on in hope? Does she apply at once for special needs help?

Perhaps the situation is not unlike imagining pupils as having electrical circuits. Some lucky pupils have their circuits completed before they arrive at school. Some have most circuits completed, leaving a few loose wires, which can be attached by trial and error. Some have lots of loose wires. These cannot be connected correctly by trial and error very easily. The sensible thing to do would be to send for a qualified electrician to help.

Another way of looking at the situation would be to

suppose that all pupils beginning school were foreigners. The school chooses a language through which most can understand. Most do so but some do not. It is not a lot of good going over the course again using the same language. Again it would be wise to find someone with experience with these children and ask for help. The teachers need help in the early stages more than do the children.

Unfortunately, it is said, a horse always unseats its rider; never does a rider just fall off. In the same way, children are said to have learning difficulties, never is the organisation or the teaching material at fault.

It would be a simple matter if all pupils needed was 'topping up'. Going over the course again can work for some of the slower learners but it merely confuses ones who have a different turn of intellect. Pupils having these needs will be enumerated in the first chapter, but to give a simple example: some people are left-handed. This does not mean that they are different in matters of learning except that they need a certain consideration. Often they need special implements to help them. Left-handedness does not affect the ability to learn to read but some intellects are affected by certain ways of teaching as will be explained.

Pupils learning to read are, as it were, sailing down a river of rapids on a raft from which twenty per cent fall off and need to be rescued. This book explains what to do.

CHAPTER ONE

The wrecking rocks of learning to read

This chapter identifies some of the 'rocks' which can wreck a pupil's learning to read. There are many factors that can prevent a child from learning to read, most of them listed as needs for learning that do not happen.

Needs for learning to read

MATURITY AND HEALTH

Initially it is important for a child to be mature enough in areas needed for learning to read. If a child cannot tell the difference between different letters or words he will not be able to progress. Equally, if his health causes him to be unable to sit still and concentrate long enough to tell which is a cow or a horse in a picture, or what else is happening, he will not be ready to learn to read. Thus a child of four could be ready in these and other respects, while another child of six may not be fully ready.

UNDERSTANDING AND INTEREST

Much learning depends upon understanding and interest.

If a child is able to understand a picture and what letters and words represent, and he is interested, then he is on the way to learning. The more interest and curiosity a child generates, the more chance he has to learn. This depends, to some extent, on intelligence and the ability to think, work things out and extrapolate and, by building answers, work out others. Understanding depends a great deal upon how information, relevant to the situation, is imparted. It needs to coincide with the pupil's level of interest as well as his past accumulated information. Much, therefore, depends upon the teachers' understanding and knowledge of the pupil. A typical instance would be where a teacher tells a pupil to look at the letter at the front of the word. The pupil can be confused because there is no way of telling that he knows which is the front or the back. Cars have headlights. People have faces. A word does not indicate a front or a back. To learn it is useful to have a teacher who understands what a pupil knows, and does not assume without making sure.

It is important for a pupil to have adequate faculties for learning to read

Obviously, a pupil needs sufficient intelligence. Even children well below average intelligence can learn to read. They may not be able to grasp the total meaning of some written work but they understand enough to be able to live decent lives. Adequate faculties would include an ability to see and hear well enough to be able to note letters and words. Those who have their sight or hearing damaged in some way need skilled assistance. Those whose sight or hearing is very out of phase with the normal are, usually, easier to recognise and allowed for; those whose sight and/or hearing is only slightly out of phase may be virtually ignored. These are they who, for a variety of reasons, make up the twenty per cent inadequate reader numbers, as will be illustrated.

Opportunity

It may be sad to say that some pupils have much more opportunity to progress than others. Often it is the children who are fortunate to have parents who realise that their child is in need of skilled assistance but often do not recognise how or why this is needed, but some make a fuss on behalf of the child who then receives help.

Some are fortunate enough to have facilities available and are intelligent enough to be able to help. It is those who are not so fortunate who contribute largely to the inadequate reader numbers.

It is those who have the opportunity, the intelligence, the pushy parents, the final motivation and interest, who manage to overcome the problems and succeed in spite of all that is done to make them into failures.

Perhaps one last need could be termed example

If a child sees a loved parent doing something that seems particularly pleasing and which is undertaken on a regular basis, the child may want to do likewise. Often the child discovers a similar talent, having inherited the co-ordination and intellectual set. As a result the example becomes much more. Often it is the persistent regularity that paves the way to success.

The wrecking rocks of learning to read

There are many ways that can prevent a child from learning to read, mostly listed as needs that have not been fulfilled. Thus parents can inadvertently prevent a child from maturing in areas needed for learning to read by ignoring letters and their uses as well as ignoring common words, such as '**STOP**' written on the road. They may never explain things or bother to look at pictures and ask questions. Some children rarely put things in order of colour, size or shape. They never handle tiny things. No wonder that it takes a good year to mature sufficiently.

Some large rocks which wreck learning are those placed in the way of a child's personal evaluation of himself. See the seven rules of rescue to follow.

Some head teachers, in the past, have persuaded parents not to teach their children to learn to read but to leave it to the school. The theory was that this would prevent the children from becoming confused – learning one way at home and another at school. This is a stumbling block but without any help at home the children learn nothing to do with reading, and have no practice looking at letters and words. They are therefore well behind others in their class. Teachers should be able to adapt to any method and not confuse the pupils into thinking that there is only one way to learn to read.

A large wrecking rock is created when a school insists on sticking to an approach that does not work for a pupil, illustrated by the fact that he does not learn. The error is then compounded by putting him through the same course again, instead of changing the approach.

A further wrecking rock is created when a pupil does not learn to read well enough to keep up with his average classmates. This shows that he has some problem that needs resolving. If it is ignored he will founder. He may be wrecked by the DO (drop out) factor, to be explained later.

The most difficult circumstances are those that remain unrecognised, causing a pupil's learning to be wrecked. Pupils with easily recognisable symptoms, such as chronic deafness or very poor sight, can be dealt with through existing organisations. It is those who experience less obvious differences from the average whose learning needs are left to struggle over the rocks. Teachers have almost no assistance in the recognition of those needs. The pupils themselves cannot explain except by not learning. This is an automatic signal indicating that the present situation is not the right one. It is true that a number of pupils do not learn to read when expected because they missed a particularly important element for some reason. The teacher has no way of knowing exactly what happened. So, to give the pupil every chance, he is put through the course again. This works for a number of pupils but serves only to confirm in others their non-understanding. Obviously the problem is to distinguish who would benefit from a repeat prescription and who would need something different. Both need to learn to read, which means encountering the same elements, but, like left-handers, one needs a different approach and maybe different materials to help. It is no help to go blundering on saying, 'All is being done that can be done,' and doing nothing more.

Dyslexia and DTT

Dyslexia in its worst form is quite rare but there are many pupils who appear to have trouble, either with visual or auditory recognition of letters or words which may be called dyslexic-type tendencies (DTT). These pupils find the recognition and remembering of letters and words unusually hard. For some it may be that they have not learnt their letters well enough. Many teachers do not teach letter names. Good readers pick them up along the way and poorer readers are left out. The letter phase, called the lexical route, is an essential element in the reading process.

Without knowing letters and their place in making up words, pupils cannot progress very far. Unfortunately, if a pupil misses this phase or only touches upon it, it is never taught or thought relevant in later stages of school learning. The knowledge is presumed to be known. If not, 'Go away and learn your letters,' is ordered. The pupil, however, has no idea how to do this, so the admonition does not help.

Academic tests tell what a pupil cannot do, they do not say how to put things right.

The drop-out (DO) factor

This factor does not affect pupils younger than almost eight years old. It is pupils who become socially aware of their need for the approval of their classmates to uphold their self-esteem. This happens at around the age of eight years. Sometimes a pupil finds that his friends are all able to read but, for some reason, he is lagging behind to such an extent that he is losing face with his friends. The usual answer is for him to say that nobody can be good at everything and he tries to find something else that he can be good at to uphold his self-esteem. The usual choice is football but, if this is out of the question, there are many other activities that can do just as well. Some ploys undertaken have been to be the worst boy in the school; the most daring girl; the best shoplifter.

All this happens because the pupil has struck a blockage in his learning to read which has not been cleared. It may not even have been noticed.

This is when the DO factor takes over. The pupil illustrates that he can do other things, so he could learn to read if he wanted, but now he does not want to. Learning to read is treated as a joke. He goes through the motions but learns nothing. There is nothing that the teacher can do as far as teaching is concerned. It is the social factor that has to be overcome and, of course, the probable DTT blockage.

The DO factor is one of the most dangerous conditions for a teacher to have to deal with. It has been overcome by moving the pupil to another school and dealing with his blockage. If the pupil continues in his chosen strain, he will almost certainly join the ranks of the great inadequate reader brigade.

It is the more intelligent pupils who are caught in the DO factor cage. Many become gang leaders and can entice other poor readers of less intelligence to join their gangs. Rarely, if ever, do hard workers become caught by the DO factor.

Emotional disturbance

All the tests and teaching effort to help a pupil to learn can be in vain if a pupil is emotionally disturbed. It is useful, therefore, to know the signs. If the pupil continues without treatment there can be lasting damage. If a pupil is suspected of being emotionally disturbed an educational psychologist should be contacted at once.

Many emotionally disturbed pupils have previously learnt well which encourages a teacher to go on trying to teach but the pupil's learning seems to hit the buffers. The pupil will appear to be quite good and promising one day and hopeless the next. Such inconsistency is one of the best indicators of the condition. Further information on this subject will be discussed in the next chapter.

Seven rules of rescue

There are times when adults can affect a pupil adversely by their attitude, behaviour and words. It has been said that the world is an unkind place and to try to shield a child from every unpleasant situation is to show an unreal world. Nevertheless, it is the job of the education service to teach a child to read. To create situations that make a pupil's learning more difficult is, surely, stupid. There are occasions which occur in a school and turns of phrase that are used which can seem convenient and for the ultimate good of the pupil but which can be the opposite. The following seven rules are listed to show the need for further thought. Much good teaching can be negated by unthinking actions and words.

1) Always ensure that a pupil's prestige and self-esteem is safeguarded. These are often dismissed as irrelevant, mostly by those with guilty consciences? Many examples could be given but two should suffice.

> The teacher is asking questions round the class. It is certain that one boy will not know the answer but he is asked. The class and the teacher laugh, as usual, when he cannot answer. A good reader is then asked and praised for the correct reply. This does nothing to help the poor reader. He learns nothing except to hate reading and, perhaps the teacher. It lowers his already low self-esteem and his classmate prestige is damaged.

See the DO factor referred to earlier.

> Another typical and common example can be seen when a teacher has a spare five minutes at the end of a lesson, an ideal time for 'flash' cards. A card is held up for the identification of a letter or word. Sometimes a poor reader is asked. Of course he does not know because the teacher never points out any points of identification or differences between similar letters or words. A good reader calls out the answer and is praised. Again, the poor reader learns nothing. His self-esteem is lowered and his prestige damaged. Before embarking on a course of action it is worthwhile to think of the possible effect it will have on the poorer readers.

2) A pupil should not be made to miss a favourite lesson or game in order to have an extra reading lesson. It may seem sound sense but is psychologically poor thinking. A typical instance of this happening would be on a Friday afternoon when the class is playing games or having a craft lesson. The pupil is given convenient extra reading lessons.

3) Special work by a pupil undertaken on behalf of a special needs teacher should be followed up by the class teacher. This may be vital practice needed for the pupil to catch up.

4) All elementary work needed to be given to a pupil which, if seen by classmates, could be demeaning for the pupil, should be undertaken in private and on a one-to-one basis. This will safeguard the pupil's prestige. An example would be when a pupil needs help in learning letters, thought by classmates to be 'baby stuff'.

5) A pupil should be given constant evidence of improvement.

6) Every effort should be made to resolve a pupil's reading problems before the age of eight. The need is to look carefully at whether a present approach is having an effect.

7) Parents should be asked to help with reading practice on a regular and consistent basis.

Conclusion

When pupils do not learn to read as expected, there are a great many reasons. Some are obvious but many are not. One needs to know these reasons, otherwise overcoming the non-learning is guesswork. If this is so, it could be wrong as well as being inefficient, lazy and a case of mis-education. This chapter indicates some causes of pupils' non-learning of reading. They are not all the reasons, for pupils have an ingenious way of compounding more methods of confounding teachers than can usually be imagined.

Some non-learning stems, in part, from the pupils' own immaturity; some from the pupils' inability to keep up with the speed of progress of the majority. Some is caused by the pupils' personal brain adjustments and anomalies, in the same way as some people are left-handed (although this has no bearing on learning-to-read ability). Some causes of lack of learning to read are caused by teachers' wrong choice of method for that pupil. Some, unwittingly, cause further havoc by choosing the wrong behaviour for that pupil.

What to do about it follows in the next chapter.

CHAPTER TWO

Riding the rapids of learning to read

Teaching a class of pupils to learn to read is like being in charge of a raft sailing down a river full of rapids. There are large rocks, small ones, some hidden, so that twenty per cent of the pupils fall off and need to be rescued.

In order to begin sorting out ways of finding what to do to eliminate the twenty per cent of inadequate readers in our schools, does one start with a rescue operation or is it better to make sure that no more fall off? LEAs believe in rescue because pupils are in that position and can be seen to need help. It would be sensible to make sure that no more are constantly being added to the number so that gradually, they decrease. So, priority should be to prevent trouble, but all the time dealing with as many 'rescues' as possible. The latter are much more difficult to deal with because pupils have had time to become used to the situation and, indeed, some will have learnt to compensate, as will be illustrated.

As there are more 'rescues' needed, they will be dealt with first. In any case, much of the material has a bearing on the prevention aspect, as will be seen.

Initially then, the teacher wants to find out why the pupil is not learning to read.

This is the diagnostic phase.

Diagnosis

Diagnosis means finding out the pupils' needs and supplying them, rather than just discovering what they cannot do.

Being a young child there are, obviously, many things that a pupil cannot do. It is no good to discover that he cannot do something and presume that this is the cause of the inability. Much depends upon the pupil's age. The older he is the longer he has had to live with his inability to learn to read. As a result many points of disturbance may have been added to his condition. An older pupil will have half come to terms with the problem. He feels that he is not good at learning to read. He may have lost interest completely. Most pupils can be redeemed once given a viable reason. The younger the pupil the easier it is to make a certain rescue. The reasons for non-learning are many.

Basically they can be classified:

1) A slow start due to immaturity of reading faculties. Some pupils hang on to this un-readiness because of other problems.
2) A problem in one or more areas, either visual or auditory.
3) Previous teaching that has been wrong for this pupil. As a result he may believe that this is the only way to learn to read. He is not good at it because of 1 or 2. Or other problems.

4) He may have compensated for his inability and refuse to learn to read.

5) Dyslexia or DTT. This causes additional teaching problems. Low intelligence does not come into it. He may be slower to learn but some have other problems such as 1, 2 or DTT.

6) Many pupils have a mixture of particularly 1, 2 and 5.

7) Missed learning.

8) No desire to read. Father could not read.

There are many reasons why this is so but, traditionally, it is presumed that the pupil has missed something or that he has not understood. The result is that he is, automatically, put through the course again. There is no attempt to find out why he cannot keep up. In fact it is very necessary to find out. It may be that he has just not understood one simple area, so going over the course again is a waste of time. It maybe that the pupil just cannot learn by the method being used, so going on trying to teach in the same way is again a waste of time. Further to this, he may have DTT, which means that he needs a different approach and more specialised assistance such as individual attention. It could be putting the pupil back considerably by trying to push him through where he cannot go, causing him to 'drop out' of learning to read altogether. To put the pupil through a test of some sort would seem the obvious thing to do.

Tests and assessments

Tests can be useful but they can be time-consuming and expensive. They also tend to accentuate the negative. One can find a hundred things that a pupil cannot do. Only a few may be relevant concerning his ability to learn to read. There may be as many as twenty tests which could give some useful information. It is often better for the teacher to devise a personal number of ways of finding out required information. This needs knowledge. Teachers are always devising their own ways of finding out and making judgements. To do so for reading assessment takes a little more thought. To discover if a pupil is able, first of all, to recognise those letters the same as those in a word just seen and not recognised. It is no good messing about with shapes which have nothing to do with letters. A quick personal trial test should satisfy this question. Try similar letters and then the same letters within words. E.g. Find a letter the same as this: t, l, t, f. Then go on to the recognition of similar words: pig, peg, dig, pig. Then ask: which of these would you live in? Horse, hose, house.

In this way the teacher is able to evaluate the pupil's ability with letter and word recognition, as well as his visual capacity, and as well as giving the pupil some practice.

Teachers might be helped by knowing something about the pupil's interests. Good ability with drawing and painting would suggest interest in details. This could mean that he would perhaps be good visually. He would be likely to be better at a look/say approach. No interest in art or pictures or dress details would suggest poor ability with look/say. Further testing would be needed, of course.

Elimination

Try to eliminate as many possibilities as can be worked out.

All the bigger ones such as deafness and poor sight should already have been checked but it might be worth double-checking. Emotional disturbance and dyslexia will be discussed later.

Poor memory

Many educational psychologists' reports say that a pupil has a poor short-term memory. Usually the pupil is tested for his memory of shapes. Young pupils are not used to the situation and often do not do very well. They do not look at the shapes well enough and have no idea how to remember them. It is the pupil's visual recognition and memory area which is affected. He has not needed such skills previously. The teacher knows from the report that the pupil will need a lot of practice in the visual area, in any case.

There seems little point in practising the recognition of shapes instead of letters when letter recognition is required. The teacher needs to indicate differences between two letters at first. Increase the number to five eventually. The difference between the letters b and d can be remembered if the word 'bed' is written and studied.

Memory difficulties may involve more than one method of recall. Thinking and talking at the same time may be difficult when trying to tell what is seen in a picture. Trying to put things in sequence or order is harder if the pupil is asked to say at the same time why things have been chosen. Again there may be difficulty in motor memory when trying to copy words from one adjacent sheet. Some pupils have to look at each letter, write it, find the word again and remember which is the next letter. It is a very slow task especially if letters are not known well. It takes some practice, encouragement and help before a pupil is able to remember a whole sequence of letters and write them. Anger from the teacher is no help.

It is vitally important for teachers to make sure that they conform with the seven rules of rescue discussed in the last chapter. It is useless trying to diagnose what to do for a pupil and to supply his needs, when his self-esteem and peer prestige is being damaged every day.

Dyslexia

A pupil who is a chronic dyslexic will be unable to see letters or words clearly. Fortunately such people are quite rare but they can still learn to read providing the right means is found for them to do so. Some dyslexics can be helped by the use of Irlen lenses, developed by the Irlen Institute in London. Some may be helped by coloured overlays. Some, again, may find that some electrical apparatus for ordering brain patterns may help them to see letters and words more plainly. These means do not help all dyslexics, so much work still needs to be done to find a means to help others.

It is reasonable to suppose that there could be others whose dyslexic symptoms are not so chronic. Their brain patterns may need less adjustment and ordering. These people place 'experts' in a quandary for by their criteria these people cannot be called dyslexic. Nevertheless these pupils do tend to find the recognition of letters and words somewhat more difficult than others. For this reason they have been placed within a category called 'dyslexic type tendencies' (DTT). The whole point of this is to give these pupils some point of rescue. It is useless guessing that all they need, and all they will get anyway, is another dose of the same course as before, which did no good then.

Co-ordination, maturity and confidence

Many DTT pupils do not co-ordinate their hand/eye actions very well and are untidy with their writing. This can improve with considerable practice. It may be that this area is less mature so that improvement takes time. If this is so, then the area may carry with it slow maturity in visual and auditory recognition of letters/words. Indeed, many pupils take a cursory glance at letters/words and then hope to guess them. This is an immature reaction. Patient practice is needed with letters, in particular. It is usually presumed that these are known and no practice is ever given. That is why it is vital that such practice should be done in private and on a one-to-one basis. See the seven rules of rescue.

Many older pupils with mild DTT illustrate this tendency in their reading by being slow. Letters and words are still muddled and the same line is read twice or one is missed out. How often does a teacher tell a pupil to read a question twice to make sure it is understood?

Helpful action

A simple early test for poor co-ordination that needs practice, and that can give a lot of information in this area, is to see if a child is able to catch a ball. The exercise needs to be graded using a large ball and a gentle toss, working up to a small ball and a longer distance thrown.

Another simple test is to roll a ball along the ground to

a sitting pupil who should try to stop the ball on a line. Again, this exercise should be graded. Start with a large ball and a gentle roll and advance to a small ball and a longer distance. Then stop the ball first with one hand and then the other. Some daily practice, lots of patience and encouragement should help improvement. It could help maturity and expertise in several directions.

Distress signals

A pupil, who by all indications of general ability and intelligence should be able to read well but is not, is signalling that something is wrong. After eliminating all major possibilities, what is left is that the pupil has some form of DTT. It has to be to do with weak recognition in either visual or auditory or both areas. The possibilities are that he needs more practice within the lexical or letter area. This is the basis of all reading learning.

The alphabetic approach

Many pupils become bogged down between visual and the auditory recognition and use of words. One way of overcoming this is for the pupil to learn the letter names which are always consistent. It is far easier to recognise the word 'out' by saying the letter names than trying to build it with letter sounds.

The simplest way to start is by learning the letter names of the vowels: a, e, i, o, u. This can prove worthwhile for medium readers who can struggle with words having two vowels together. In many such words the sound is the same as the name of the first vowel, e.g. seat, coat. The same applies to words ending in e, e.g. cake, wine, mole. That the rule does not apply in every case does not matter for pupils, usually, are able to guess the word.

To learn other letter names the teacher is able to boost the pupil's confidence by pointing out that he knows a lot of them already. Try to find some of them. BBC, ITV, BMW, p for pence, OK, and many more. Suggest the idea of sending secret messages such as: I see you are too wise to use tea, written as I c ur yy uu t.

Further Rescue

Many pupils are at a stage where they have become two or more years behind their average classmates in reading. They have tried and found, from the experience of several years, that reading is something that they are not good at. Some, about age eight-plus to nine, have embraced the DO factor and have compensated for the inability. Suppose that now their social situation has changed. The teacher wants to know why this otherwise capable pupil is not reading. It is a case of neglected DTT. The trouble is, obviously, either in the visual or the auditory area or even both. If the pupil has been taught using the phonic method for some time, the teacher might suspect that this approach does not fit. Test this supposition first of all. Listen to his attempt at reading. This should be a useful guide. Note, in particular, his expertise with letter and word recognition. Test knowledge of letter names using games to gain information. Games of chance are helpful, especially if the teacher can cheat a little in favour of the pupil but not too often.

It is considerably more useful to have a one-to-one

relationship for perhaps twenty minutes, rather than to have a group all afternoon, or even three together for an hour. Nobody is distracted and the pupil has to work non-stop and concentrate, which may be unusually hard work for some. The teacher too can learn a lot more quickly.

Use games again to determine recognition of words. Older pupils in need of letter/word recognition practice have been asked to make cards for younger pupils.

All the time the teacher is trying to see if there is a requirement for visual or auditory preference for the pupil's learning needs. Concentrate initially on good knowledge of letters and then on word build-up. Note the expertise with the knowledge of vowels and their use. Suggest how to deal with the sound of two vowels together. Note improvement and point it out.

Occasionally a pupil may have an opportunity to help another pupil with something that has just been learnt. This may be one of the ways to reinforce learning.

The final thing would be for the pupil to have some reading practice every day. This is an area where parents can assist. See suggestions in Chapter Seven.

It can be a good idea in rescue work to discard the present method used and not to teach the same way to a pupil who has plainly not succeeded with what has been offered before. Take on the use of the old alphabetic approach, e.g. 'o.u.t' spells 'out'. This, of course, depends on the pupil knowing the letter names, which, as pointed out, are not difficult to learn. This can cut most of the word building by sound. Strangely enough, some pupils have good memories for these consistent letter names and the ring they can give to a word.

See the chapter on spelling.

Prevention

The prevention of a pupil from becoming poor at reading is something that has to be undertaken early in the pupil's school life. One can understand why an education authority is reluctant to deal with the prevention of such problems. Looking at it from the raft in the rapids aspect, if one spent money safeguarding certain pupils by giving them a handle to hang on to, how can one explain that the pupil would have fallen off without it? True, he might not have fallen off but it is better to make sure. Education authorities are not keen on possibilities. They need to say to financial departments that there are x number of pupils in x number of schools who are poor readers and something has to be done.

So, it seems, it is up to the teachers, and this book, to try to make sure that the pupils who are likely to fall off the learning-to-read raft do not do so. Rescue pupils are unmistakably there to see. Prevention pupils cannot be seen so easily by others. The teacher knows that, for some pupils, it would be a miracle if they suddenly began to learn to read. The majority will manage it eventually by dint of hard work all round, but some will not because they have DTT, making the teacher's job more difficult. Methods and approaches have to be found to fit these pupils. This needs a lot of extra work and foresight on the teacher's part. This has to be anticipated and worked out without any advice or assistance. It would be much easier to ignore these DTT pupils, let them 'fall off', and then try to rescue them. This would naturally be much harder to accomplish.

Prevention has to be accomplished before the pupil is age eight years. Initially the teacher is faced with a five-year-old, immature in the areas needed for learning to read. Much work needs to be done to push on the child's maturity. This is standard work in many primary schools. It is not so standard for prevention. Teachers know that numbers of these pupils come from homes where reading is not the usual occupation. Talking often consists of shouted orders and loud arguments. School is a different life. The teachers are expected to introduce and lead pupils through a maze of language and behaviour which is strange, hard work, and often seems meaningless. No wonder it takes some pupils more than a year to grasp the intentions. Fortunately, most pupils want to keep up with their friends and are intelligent enough to be able to do so. It needs pounds of patience on the teacher's part. It is hard enough when the pupil's faculties are about normal. Trouble comes when a pupil has DTT even mildly. His reactions appear to suggest that his intelligence is low whereas it may be at least average. Further tests would give a better clue. The need is to confirm or deny the presence of DTT. Test visual and auditory reactions, strengths and abilities. This will give a guide as to how to begin teaching reading. It would be unkind to try to push the auditory sound of letters/words if it was obvious that this was the pupil's weakest area.

Begin so that the pupil has the most chance of success instead of always being wrong, i.e. do not use 'flash cards' to illustrate a good reader's superiority. This belittles a poorer reader. Explain points of recognition and similarity.

Story outlines

Explain and illustrate how a DTT pupil can help himself by hanging on to any 'handles' that can be found, i.e. using context cues. It would be useful, particularly for DTT pupils for the teacher to point out ways of discovering the general outline of a story. Any pictures should always give a clue. Show how the story is set out. This can be very useful for finding out words. Good readers pick this up themselves but DTT readers need these 'handles' to help them. Context cues need finding so it is not just deciphering one word after another.

The teacher needs to make sure that the pupil understands whatever is taught. Never presume that the pupil knows something because it has been taught. Work out a quick revision to check.

Many DTT pupils find that they need to work harder than others in order to keep up. He therefore needs constant encouragement.

Special Sessions

It may be necessary for some DTT pupils to have a regular twenty-minute individual special session every week on a one-to-one basis from the age of six onwards. In this way he will be well on his way to reading at age eight years.

Would he have been reading at age eight without this special care? The teacher knows very well that he would not. There would be no congratulations.

Extra help

Not every reception teacher would be able to follow the above suggestions for preventing a pupil becoming a case for rescue. Many a time when a pupil is between the age of seven to eight, a teacher will say that a 'breakthrough' is expected daily but, alas, nothing happens. The teacher is at a loss to understand why. Everything possible has been done, it is said.

The LEA could help by appointing a qualified and knowledgeable person with a simple brief, namely, to prevent children reaching the secondary schools as non-readers. Each such person appointed might be given between twelve and twenty schools to look after, according to their size. Such a person would help the teachers to rescue vulnerable pupils and prevent predictable difficulties. The LEA would see a vast improvement within three years. Hopefully, this person could then move on to another area or a wider group. Of course, some would say that the area was a more middle-class area where such reading problems rarely existed. Nobody ever falls off if they have enough sense and the teachers are experts?

Emotional Disturbance

Pupils having emotional disturbances are not always easy to discover. They may have learnt well previously so teachers may expect work to be as good. Emotionally disturbed pupils are inconsistent. There are a number of pointers. For instance: a pupil may know the four-times-table well but be unable to work out how many legs three cows would have altogether. Such a pupil could be quite promising one day and hopeless the next. Other signs are:

➢ Hyperactivity or passivity
➢ Ultra talkativeness
➢ Inability to delay gratification
➢ Restless and distractible
➢ Extreme attention seeking
➢ Over-familiarity
➢ Erratic and uninhibited outbursts

Emotionally disturbed children have, generally, a number of consistent difficulties. The following may be useful to test suspicions:

➢ Difficulty in finding the meaning of pictures.
➢ Difficulty in reproducing patterns.
➢ Difficulty in finding a hidden object in a picture. Make sure that the pupil is not colour blind, i.e. cannot tell the difference between red and green.
➢ Difficulty in stopping an activity.
➢ Difficulty in making groups of similar things, as in mathematics.
➢ Untidy work due to muscle unco-ordination.
➢ Often seeks the company of much younger children.
➢ Tends to disrupt games of others.
➢ Hates being corrected and often becomes truculent.

Such pupils can often say and remember poems, lists of facts, birthdays, etc. but cannot use the information. They love lists and repeat patterns.

Some pupils have a number of these signs but after a while they disappear, so it is not so easy to be certain. It may be a good idea to talk to these pupils about their life and what worries them. If the signs are regular and consistent, an educational psychologist should be informed and asked to check. Considerable damage could be done if such disturbed pupils are left. Rescue is up to the educational psychologist.

Bullying

Bullying is an aspect of school life that is often hard to stop because it happens when teachers are not there. However, if it continues for some time indications become ever more obvious. Bullies themselves are maladjusted rather than being emotionally disturbed. They enjoy the primitive emotion of feeling control over another person, usually smaller and not so strong. This feeling is fed by bullying. This may be the result of experiencing frustrations and failure. The wish to be good at something and to demonstrate it to the 'gang' can be quite overpowering, as it can be with those who embrace the 'drop out' factor, previously explained. This is often the result of an unresolved DTT situation.

Bullies need to be rescued as much as anyone else but they are in a much more difficult position. The primitiveness of their unkind actions need to be pointed out to the 'gang' so that they are not tempted to follow. When the bully finds out that his actions do not gain admiration, the whole action loses attraction.

Those who are bullied, initially, have several trial answers. Bullies require an easy target. If the person chosen makes the bullying operation hard work and not very satisfying, then the bully will tend to give up and try someone else. It is worth it to fight back, in some way. It is always useful for smaller people to have big friends. There is then no need to say or do anything.

It is worthwhile to let bullies know that their actions leave their 'signature' without anyone saying anything. Teachers need to watch for poor work, frightened looks, absenteeism and withdrawal signs from those suffering bullying.

Conclusion

In a pupil's learning situation, every reaction illustrates a need either for him or for the teacher. If just half of these needs are ignored then the pupil will not progress very well. The act of teaching requires that the pupil should learn. All the time the teacher should be probing, eliciting reactions to the teaching and the pupil's understanding. It is no good if a teacher just 'spouts' material and does not bother to read any reactions. Reading material is only useful if the pupil understands it. There is little point in teaching if the teacher is just a book.

Diagnosis, then, is ongoing. If understanding is not there it would be sensible to check the basic roots first. In learning to read, the basic roots stem from the letters. If one way is not taken in, try another but the pupil must know his letters, or, at least, enough of them to enable him to read. There is little need to go through elaborate tests for everything. The pupil will not be able to do a hundred things but only a few will really be relevant and the teacher can, quite often, find out by using a personal trial test/exercise.

After this, a pupil's personal faculties come next. It is useful for a teacher to know which faculties give a pupil his abilities and to try to utilise these as much as possible. Sometimes a pupil's learning, even in his best area, visual or auditory, is so 'sticky' that continual, regular and consistent practice is the only answer. The secret is in the regularity, not the amount. See Chapter Seven.

To rescue a pupil who has fallen off the learning-to-read raft is what every teacher would want. To prevent him from falling off should be the object, not only of the reception teacher but also the school and the LEA in a combined effort. It is possible and it has been done.

CHAPTER THREE

Mapping a route down the learning to read river rapids

It is wise to map a route down a river with rapids so that some hazards may be avoided. In learning to read there can be many snags, many unforeseen. Head teachers always pick a way that they believe would be better for the pupils but this is for the majority. The suggestions here are for the prevention and rescue of pupils who may be vulnerable as well as others. There are many variations of methods of beginning the teaching of reading according to circumstances. As it has been said, knowledge of letters is vitally important and there are many ways of introducing them. Some teachers neglect teaching letter names. This may be fine for a class of pupils who can pick up such information on the way but it can spell disaster for those who never pick up such things.

Some teachers believe that letter names can cause confusion.

The attempt to build words by sound by pupils who have a poor sound appreciation, for instance, tends to reinforce their lack of confidence. It would be better for such pupils to use some elements of the alphabetic approach because:

➢ Letters, being small, afford an opportunity for pupils' critical recognition/differentiation practice which most pupils need.
➢ Letters have names, which can be useful, as explained previously.
➢ Work with letters may assist with visual and auditory maturity.
➢ Letter names can be used to augment phonic work.
➢ Letter names are consistent and can be used to help spelling.
➢ Remembering letter order helps sequencing and memory.
➢ Learning vowel names is a simple and easy introduction and allows immediate successful application affording a confidence boost.
➢ Letter names afford another tool ready for immediate use.
➢ Letter knowledge may be augmented by a pupil and converted to a more phonic use if required

There may be at least three ways in which meaning may be extracted from print. One development sequence describing how children learn to read is:

Stage 1. Whole words are identified through the recognition of special points in words seen before.
Stage 2. The same stage as Stage 1 but the pupils may guess from the group of known words.

Stage 3. The beginning of the recognition of words aided by a phonic build-up of a word augmented by contextual clues.

Stage 4. The use of additional aids. This may be how many pupils are taught. They need the route reinforced by the more concrete use of letters. Some teachers have been afraid that the concentration on letters would detract from the necessary quest for textual meaning but this is to presume that, as it were, driving a car round a field concentrating on clutch and gears, would detract from eventually driving well. Pupils usually have more learning capability than this.

In the New Zealand programme of rescue and prevention, letters hold an important position.

They deal with the whole situation of poor readers mainly with pupils under the age of eight years, as is advised in this book.

Book language

The difference in register between ordinary and book language needs to be explained to poor readers. The difference in the type of language used in informative books and storybooks can be very different. Indeed, many poorer readers do not like hearing stories read. They do not fully understand and become bored and 'switch off'. If this is so, it must be hard for them to understand stories they are expected to read themselves. No wonder 'the cat sat on the mat' and other boringly simplified books are sometimes initially favoured.

Exercises, i.e. a sentence written, given a choice of three meanings, each numbered, as previously explained, where the object is for the pupil to read and only to write the number of the answer, would give both teacher and pupil some help.

See chapter on comprehension to follow.

Telling tales

In order to grade story language and give poorer readers, as well as others, opportunities to practise language construction, most teachers have pupils telling their 'news' every morning. The trouble is that not everyone has a chance so, usually, only the better talkers are heard. It is suggested therefore, that three pupils are given a tape recorder and three exciting pictures – each pupil to tell a story, involving the three pictures. It does not matter if the stories are similar. What matters is that the pupils' talk is understood.

Following this the teacher would be better to tell a story, initially, rather than to read it. In this way it is soon plain if the story is getting boring so the teacher can inject some extra interest.

Such a storytelling includes facial expressions, gestures and tones of voice. A written story has none of these so the teacher, somehow, needs to create a halfway stage to illustrate that written stories too need the reader to visualise the action. This leads on to showing how the writer tries to help by including descriptions and particular words. A young reader has an enormous gap to jump. It would be sensible to try to grade the 'slope' by making various stages.

- A short simple story is told accompanied by a lively picture.
- Pupils tell the same story to others. The teacher watches and helps.
- Part of a story is told. Pupils suggest a middle when asked, 'What happened next?' Other pupils invent an ending.
- Pupils start a story aided by a picture. The teacher finishes it.
- Pupils tell the same story to others helped by the teacher who asks, 'What happened next?'
- The same story is read.
- Pupils read the same or similar story.
- Pupils listen to a short story on tape. It may be noticed that pupils stare at the teacher's face as though some meaning could be gained from it. It may be some time before it is realised that ALL the meaning is in the words. They may then understand that when reading, all the expression has to come from the reader through the words. Just telling a pupil does not have any effect.
- Make a story, using pictures, in note form to give some idea of the story. Go on working with short stories as suggested previously.
- Pupils listen to a story on tape and sequence up to seven pictures. This should be done as the story unfolds. Start with three pictures and work up to a maximum of seven as the pupils improve.

Constant revision

In both prevention and rescue terms, one consideration must

take an important position. Constant revision is vital. There is no need for a mass of detailed exam-type revision every week. All that is necessary is a few words. This is where the teacher needs to be able to précis all that has been covered and then to devise a telling question with three possible numbered answers, one being correct. The pupils practise reading but need only write a number for the answer, which is quick.

It is the regularity of such revision that matters. Just because something has been covered does not mean that it has 'stuck' in pupils' minds. Revision means giving a chance to *see again.*

It is as if the brain's object is to forget as much as possible. When it is given no opportunity to forget, then, finally it gives up and remembers.

This is where tiny step-by-step advances add up. If one small thing is hard to remember a step back makes a logical small advance logical.

Tests and exams scare many pupils but if they are merely a weekly quiz they become un-fearful and can be quite fun.

If a pupil has missed some letter-learning a change to cursive lettering will force a review. It may take some time but it could be a face-saver. At the same time many other forms of lettering might be introduced in the form of secret notes, e.g. the Treasure is hidden on island, see © under the biggest rock on the side of the sun at six o'clock. All the letters to be cut out of newspaper, typed print, and some written. A good homework exercise?

Conclusion

Fortunately there are few teachers who, when sailing their raft down the learning-to-read river of rapids, sail it as though there are no hazards. It is tempting to concentrate on the eighty per cent of pupils who are successful and ignore the twenty per cent who fall off. One might say, 'Oh, they will learn to read in their own time.' Or, 'They have specific learning difficulties and ought to be in a Special School.'

It is better to stretch out a hand of rescue rather than to throw a hopeful rope later.

Most teachers do map out a route but with a fairly constant eighty per cent success rate, it can become so routine that the twenty per cent who seem to concentrate on finding an ingenious way of slipping off without the teacher noticing can be forgotten.

When the majority consider that learning about letters is 'baby stuff', it is not easy to give such lessons to a needy twenty per cent. Some way has to be found. It is equally easy to presume that every pupil will readily understand book language because the majority show no particular bother. Some teachers are then surprised that pupils tend to 'bark at print'.

CHAPTER FOUR

Writing: another way to reading

It may be unusual to say that writing can be another way of learning to read. One obstacle, for some people, is that many poor readers also have poor hand/eye co-ordination so that their control of a pen or pencil is understandably the cause of untidy writing. It is often traditional to make a fuss and say that such a mess is not acceptable in order to make the pupil try harder with his control. It could be a waste of valuable learning time for more important elements. The object of this exercise is that pupils should love writing.

One boy was so low in his general ability that he was sent to a special school. He learnt to read and enjoyed writing so much that he went on writing letters for two years after he left school and had a job. This may be unusual but it shows that, with the right approach and encouragement, it can be done.

Pupils should be asked to write to someone other than the teacher who, usually, is seen as a criticiser. The writing is for content, not neatness or correct spelling. Encourage the pupil to have a go at words and to try to remember what it was meant to say. Do not ask a pupil to read out to the class what has been written. To do so acts like a punishment so that the pupil is discouraged from writing any more in case he is asked to read it again. It might also be off-putting if the teacher reads it aloud. To the teacher the words may be amusing such as: 'Ther wus not a clod in the ski.' For the pupil the idea was there.

Writing is completely different and a more complicated operation than speech. The difference can be a fascinating change for some pupils, especially if they find their efforts are praised rather than marked all over with spellings. If the writing or letter is treated as private and the recipient only can read it, unless the pupil asks for help, it also helps.

Writing is more abstract than the spoken word. This requires a certain discipline and sequencing ability. Skills are needed of a higher order than for reading. Writing needs to be thought out more carefully than speech, which is often hesitant and full of unnecessary words, 'you know'. Speech is transient whereas writing is much more permanent. Patience is necessary for thought making sense. This, in turn, leads to thoughts being generated, so considerable concentration is required. When thoughts are written down some order is needed and such thinking leads to character building and beliefs. There may be, theoretically, many strategies of quite complicated learning for a poor reader to pass through. While this may be true for good writing, one might be tempted to say that such expertise could not be expected of poor readers. Somehow all this does not seem to deter even a poor reader who appears to take a simplified view of this complicated operation. He may not know or understand many words but he does know his letters. Writing, then, is putting letters in an order to signify words. Initially, many words may be wrong but this is irrelevant. It is the content that matters. Pupils are practising letter and word recognition. When reading later, they come across words they had wanted to write. With practice they remember them. One of the main things a pupil has to remember is that he is writing so that someone may read it. The first point that he needs to understand is what he has written. If he does not then who else will? There should be no objection to made-up words, providing that the pupil can remember the meaning.

For the teacher the exercise is one of code breaking, for every other word may be a challenge. The trouble is that the teacher has little to show except an unmarked mess. This is not laziness, it is common sense which can be explained.

Writing a story can be very simple, consisting of a few words, as was explained in the last chapter. These few words need to be expanded by the pupil asking himself, constantly, 'What happened next?' There could be a great deal of information and description as well as writing about people's feelings and reactions.

This is, of course, making a picture with words. If an actual picture or drawing was included, it could make reading stories even more interesting.

Many children have a great imagination and enjoy telling stories. As spoken, these imaginings may be called lies but if the same stories were written, they would not be lies. Like painting a picture it is no good trying to paint every leaf on a tree. The best way is to give a good impression of the leaves. In writing, too many words can spoil a story. What is wanted is the fewest but most descriptive words.

Surrogate writing

One gradual and useful step would be for the pupil to say what was wanted but for the adult to write it. The main danger here is the adult. It is often too tempting for the adult to suggest a better way to say something. The net result is that what is written bears little resemblance to what the pupil wanted to say and he does not recognise the words. The adult needs to write most, if not all, that the pupil says. Discuss it when complete. The pupil then understands it and can ask for a better way of expressing some of the sentences. The thing that the adult needs to stress is that the pupil should say one simple thing at a time, not a whole string of sentences joined by 'and'.

When a number of these stories have been completed, bind them into a book form for other pupils to read, including the author's name. Perhaps a few illustrations could also be included.

The idea can progress to the pupil writing part of a story himself and then all of it.

It is wise not to insist that a pupil should read his stories aloud. Arrive at this stage very gradually so as not to dent confidence. Let it come from the pupil. It is often better to write a letter to a relative or friend at first and leave story-writing to a later stage for some less confident pupils.

Pupils with DTT often have poor language command. One difficulty is an inability to say and appreciate longer words. This is where cursive writing helps. The pupil feels that he has progressed. It also helps tidiness and speed.

In France children are presented with script and cursive at a very early age so that it is not such a sudden new change. Pupils learn cursive script using a uni-sensory method rather than a multi-sensory approach. This has been found to be more successful. Using a kinaesthetic approach often means that pupils need to be blindfolded because seeing and hearing prove too much of a distraction to the learning by feeling. Cursive writing often adds an improvement in spelling as well as tidiness and, of course, reversals. In addition general reading ability improves.

Initially, after being used to printing, pupils find it hard not to keep lifting the pen after each letter but this soon improves.

Writing and reading co-ordination

Particular care needs to be exercised at this stage, when reading skills are not good. Make certain that the pupil is able to recognise and differentiate all letters and similar words such as horse and house.

Without delving too much into the realms of spelling, it would be a good idea to point out that, in making words, in the same way as there are two vowels together sometimes, there can be two consonants and sometimes three but never four, except in names. After the consonant there is always a vowel. There should be one or more vowels in every word. This is something that is so obvious that it is not always noticed and leads naturally on to spelling.

Conclusion

Every story that a pupil reads was once written by someone. Often pupils do not realise this. Just as all stories were once written by someone, so could the pupils write something that, if it is very good, could be made into a book just the same. It takes a lot of patience and ingenuity for a teacher to have pupils who really enjoy writing. Reading does improve quite rapidly as pupils write. Writing can be a pleasant change from the incessant reading practice. The main object is for pupils to enjoy writing and want to continue on their own.

CHAPTER FIVE

Spelling: working with words

Learning spelling facilitates growth in reading ability. Spelling promotes insight into the alphabetic nature of written language. Spelling is related to word recognition, understanding of meaning and situation in the sentence. It is concerned, also, with particular units of speech-sound (phonemes) as each is represented by a letter or letters, (graphemes) as they are put together in words (morphemes).

If word recognition is poor, letter recognition may also be poor. To attempt to improve spelling, merely by copying words or trying to learn them by rote, probably will not succeed, as well as being boring. Nevertheless there is a need for accuracy in spelling and beginners are not accurate, especially poor readers. However, marking every spelling would probably come very low on the work advantage list.

Spelling recall

Spelling recall is the reverse of reading where one associates letters with the sound of the word and its meaning (decoding). In spelling the pupil usually tries to equate the symbols required for various sounds (encoding). In this there is often no assistance except for the pupil's past memory of the word. Transfer of this knowledge by itself to reading words results in 'sounding out' with no insight into how the sounds relate to pronunciation. The crux of the matter is knowing how to combine the letters into units appropriate for speech. There are a great many non-phonetic words in English. As a result there have been many attempts to ease the burden for children by simplifying spelling. This may have made learning to read and write a little easier but it has ruined the ability to spell. The learning of correct spelling never seems to be important enough. The result is that there are numbers of adults who still spell by using basic letter sounds. The attitude appears to be that it is better to spell in this way than not to write at all. This was the accepted idea about three hundred years ago.

Recognition of words

Writing may be distinguished from other means of visual communication because in writing the symbols correspond to units of the spoken language rather than directly expressing objects or concepts. The language spoken is recognised by the sounds that are used. In reading, automatically, the reader attempts to convey what the eye sees to represent the sound that one would recognise if the word was spoken. In many cases, therefore, a reader only requires a clue in order to be able to build the whole word. This is how good readers manage to read at an early age. Poor readers are at a disadvantage in that they do not recognise the telltale clues. They experience a similar disadvantage concerning letters in words. It is similar with people who remember faces and names of others. Good readers, when they have seen a word, recognise it visually whereas poor readers take longer to remember.

If one word is very different from another it is more easily remembered. Similar-looking words need the differences pointing out. Poor readers can often remember the spelling of 'ghost' because the 'g' is followed by 'h' for howl, if it is pointed out.

Bizarre spelling

There are pupils who, for a number of reasons, learn to read quite well but whose spelling contains what most adults call bizarre mistakes. These may be because of confusion of sound or sight. It may be not understanding the place of letters or just not knowing the letters. Some pupils begin their bizarre spelling because of some genuine confusion coupled with a desire to write without continually stopping for spellings. Sometimes a bizarre spelling is continued for attention seeking.

Those pupils who display genuine confusion and yet still try to spell by the sound build-up may know no other way. They may be helped by the alphabetic and visual approach. See following.

Those who have great difficulty in spelling although they are quite good readers, have probably learnt to read whole words by sight but have never learnt the letters by name or sound sufficiently well.

Bizarre spelling has been overcome when letter names have been learnt. There are pupils who cannot appreciate the sound build-up of words. These pupils need the use of other senses instead.

A visual approach

This approach has been found to be very helpful to poor readers. Words are split up into sections of two, three or four letters such as the following: elephant: ele ph ant; television: tele visi on; father: fat her. The split words are discussed. Ele is like an ear, a trunk and another ear, ph with a down stick and one up is right in the middle. Ant spells ant, so an eleph must be a very large ant. An even bigger one would be a giant. Tele has two ears; visi has two eyes, when it is on. Fat spells fat, so a father must be a fat her. It would not be wise to call one's father a fat her.

Pupils soon pick up the idea of splitting words in a way that they can remember; re mem ber, or rem em ber. Leaving the splitting-up to the individual gives some responsibility and independence so pupils can learn in their own way.

In this way a short list of words might be picked from the pupil's own writing that could be corrected and split up by themselves and learnt.

The use of a dictionary

Such use presumes that the pupil not only knows his letters but is familiar with letter order. This often expects too much of a poor reader and serves only to frustrate and confuse. There is no alternative to learning letter order. It can be made easier by splitting the alphabet into blocks; a-g; h-n; o-t, u-z; These blocks should be coloured for quicker identification. If the appropriate sections of the index or dictionary are also coloured, similarly, then the process could be speedier.

Spelling can be fun even for poorer readers providing some order is given to the necessary learning.

Spelling is usually under scrutiny after a pupil has written something where there are numerous mistakes. Pupils might be asked to choose five or six of these that interest them most. After correction the pupil can then split the words up and learn to spell them.

Conclusion

Spelling correctly depends upon a memory for the right letters and their sequence to be remembered. This comes with constant practice and with reading. This is helped if the pupil has an interest in good spelling. Spelling for general use may not need to be insisted upon, especially if it deters the pupil from writing. It should be of a standard able to understand. Pupils should have a pride in their ability to spell. This can only come with constant practice and a will to be right.

CHAPTER SIX

Comprehension:
understanding what is read

Understanding what has been read is so important that reading has been called comprehension. In learning from reading, sensitivity to importance of words is one of the preconditions for the ability to concentrate on parts of the text that will not be remembered automatically. If pupils are not sensitive to such importance it means that they need some practice in this area. For instance, the words 'The cat sat on the mat' can be remembered automatically. In the sentence, 'The purple cat with the blue stripe down its tail sat quite still on the rusty yellow mat,' the words cat, sat and mat are there but they are harder to pick out when so many other words are confusing the simple issue.

Naturally, a teacher wants to know if the pupil has understood what has been read but there seems little point in comprehension measurement. Reading ability can be measured so perhaps this should be enough. 'Barking at print' is a common complaint but it stems from the pupil being required to read aloud. This, in fact, may be a step ahead of a pupil's ability. He is required to recognise the words and also to 'voice' them. When reading it is not necessary to look at every word in order to recognise the sense but in reading aloud the pupil has to decipher every word and speak at the same time. In concentrating on the reading, the sense is not, seemingly, required. Then, suddenly, more than this is wanted, requiring what the words actually mean. There are two points to note. First, when one reads a text one is able to recognise the gist of the meaning but poor readers have more difficulty. If the words are alien to the pupil's thinking and the resulting language is more complicated, as is common in book language, it may be necessary to point out the salient features. Young children's concepts are very concrete and can remain so for some time. Placing ideas and concepts that are unfamiliar in their way means only the words will be read. Secondly, poor readers are often unable to use the same language as the text. This ability to interpret takes practice, which can be gained by re-telling stories heard or previously read.

Looking at comprehension from the raft on the learning-to-read river angle, it is not pupils who fall off and need to be rescued, it is more that, during the voyage, many 'nautical' terms are used, which are not understood. Pupils might have the general idea of what 'splice the main brace' means but not really understand it.

The pupil has to become used to verbalising his thoughts and arranging these and his speech somewhere near synchronisation. The teacher needs to be aware of these very real problems and be ready to offer some support, so that the pupil gains some confidence and is not afraid of ridicule.

Quite often there may be more than one meaning for a text at first. It might be helpful to supply three possible answers and ask for a forecast as to the correct meaning.

Pupils may be helped by expanding their knowledge of new words. This helps to increase a pupil's essential background knowledge.

Seeing the reading process

There is often a disadvantage for a teacher in trying to gauge whether a pupil has understood a text. When questions are asked it means that they need to be the right ones. If a pupil's background knowledge is good it is possible to answer many questions without even seeing the text. This is not likely to happen to poor readers.

The reading process itself is not observable so the teacher has to guess what is going on in the pupil's head. It is necessary to ask questions that cannot be answered merely by copying portions of the text. However, pupils cannot be expected to jump from copying text to making inferences and using their own words without some graduation in the steps, especially if they are poor readers. It would seem sensible to discuss various texts with pupils so that they realise the different ways that writers express their ideas. Pupils need to know what words are the most revealing and why they were chosen.

Discussion on the subject can be made interesting by taking a piece written by the pupil himself with his permission. This permission is essential.

A useful introductory method of discovering meaning is to use various modifications of the missing word exercise, known technically as 'cloze procedure'.

A basic problem with some comprehension is that a pupil's recognition of known information varies with pupils and materials. This, if some texts are harder to understand than others, may be because there are not sufficient cues for the pupil's understanding. Sometimes a pupil may misunderstand a single cue, which causes the whole text to be misunderstood. This is seen most often in exams, when the teacher warns to read the questions twice. A way to practise text understanding is to fill in a missing word from a choice of three words. This may be a more efficient method than asking questions. The exercise can be graded by a careful choice of word. A good reader may be given a harder choice than someone less accomplished. In this way both pupils can do the same type of work with no loss of 'face'.

Comprehension skills

- ➢ Identifying word meaning either directly or through context.
- ➢ Drawing inferences from parts of the text.
- ➢ Finding clues to main ideas.
- ➢ Making judgements concerning meanings and ideas.
- ➢ Ability to reflect on what has been read.

The efficient use of books, even for good readers, does not seem to come automatically, so there is need for clear teaching which is particularly needed for poorer readers.

Comprehension strategies

It is a good idea to read a text more than once. At first, a quick read, skimming and scanning to find any outstanding cues to have a rough idea of what the text is about. Then a more careful read to confirm the first impression. Then a final read, perhaps to précis the text.

Besides the ability to employ commonsense strategies such as noting the sequence of ideas, the pupil needs to be able to consider the possible outcomes and the result of cause and effect. He needs to note that often a writer tries to make his ideas so realistic that there is no need to gauge what is fiction and what is really fact. This is more necessary at an older level of understanding but young pupils should realise that this can be good writing rather than making up lies. It is a writer's strategy, as mentioned in a previous chapter. So what is read in a newspaper may not necessarily be the accurate truth all the time.

Working towards understanding

- ➢ Materials should be used which are conceptually familiar to pupils for the most part.
- ➢ Attempt to increase pupils' background knowledge.
- ➢ Allow pupils copious practice with thought expression.
- ➢ Pupils should be helped to find main ideas in texts and be sensitive to the relative importance of other parts.
- ➢ Pupils need help to make inferences concerning the text and to make judgements.
- ➢ Pupils will need help in assessing the probability of fact and fiction.
- ➢ Pupils need help with the use of pronouns to shorten texts.
- ➢ Pupils need help to be able to speculate on outcomes and to recognise assumptions.

Conclusion

When pupils are beginning to learn to read, comprehension is, generally, not considered. 'The cat sat on the mat' type of reading would not provoke anxiety regarding understanding, if it was considered. It is much later, when pupils begin rattling off the words, when they are then challenged to give the meaning. Many stories are so mundane that they could hardly be expected to gather much interest from a pupil. As a result there is little incentive to want to know what happened.

In the old days boys' magazine stories may have been trash when compared with classics, but they caught the interest and helped at least one poor reader to improve.

A teacher needs to be good to help a pupil improve with his comprehension. It would be a great help to begin by capturing the pupils' interest.

CHAPTER SEVEN

Homework

Looking at the situation of the twenty per cent of inadequate readers from the viewpoint of a raft on the learning-to-read river of rapids, good readers are in the middle whereas poor readers are along the sides and likely to fall off. Not everyone can be in the middle but those who are on the sides can be safeguarded from falling off. The home, where considerable time is spent outside of school hours, can help a great deal.

Poor readers often have weak motivation to learn to read. This, in addition to possible dyslexic-type tendencies and a general struggle for more advanced maturity, all cause the child to want to spend more time at play.

When school begins weekends and holidays are times for forgetting. This is a time when the home can help. Given time to forget, the young brain does so with alacrity. The home atmosphere can help. If there are older children, they can give a good lead even if they do not want to help. Often a younger child wants to keep up with an older brother or sister.

Poor readers' families sometimes make the excuse that the child will learn to read in good time and anyway it is the job of the school not theirs.

Home/school liaison

There are a number of ways in which a school reception teacher can prepare for a child just beginning school. It would be useful to make an introductory visit to the home. This can have a number of advantages. It shows that the teacher is human and friendly, as well as being interested in the child. It is better than having a person calling at the school. All the feelings are more towards the home because it is theirs while the school is on 'opposition' ground. This can be quite important. It makes the possible 'nosiness' of the teacher less in evidence when she can talk about the prospective pupil and his interests. The teacher has to be careful not to jump to conclusions, which might be wrong if the child does not want to show off how well learning to read is progressing. The teacher can have a good idea of the child's maturity level and willingness to learn. She can advise on how the home can help without being too dictatorial.

An initial guideline pamphlet by way of introduction may be useful, along the following lines:

> ➢ Pick up a child's book and talk about the cover, the picture and the author. Listen to what the child has to say.
> ➢ Read some of a story. Try to find a bit that is exciting, making the child want to know what happened next.

> ➤ If the child is able to read a little, do not keep correcting him especially if he has the general meaning right.
> ➤ When the child is stuck over a word do not immediately give it. Go back and ask if he can guess it, given the initial letter. Get him to build a bit of it and have another try. Alternatively, miss the word and go on reading saying the word 'something' instead and then go back at the end of the sentence. See if reference to a picture or previous information could help.
> ➤ When the story is finished talk about it. Was it as expected? Do not ask questions that need a right answer. This is a time for enjoyment, not for testing. Discuss what was liked or disliked and find out why. Perhaps retell the story or part of it. How did it relate to the child, his experiences or expectations? Talk about feelings and characters. Were they kind, unkind, happy or unhappy?

A poor reader's home may never think of asking such questions about stories. Some children may never have thought in this way.

Changing Lifestyles

In asking for the co-operation of the home in the education of their children, it often means that schools are requesting a complete change of lifestyle. The home needs to be convinced that such a drastic change is really worthwhile, if this is possible. Teachers, therefore, need to be sensible and realistic, and not make suggestions that are not possible. Strict consistency may not always fit in with daily working.

The school needs to remember this and not blame the pupil all the time. A personal talk with whomever runs the home would help.

Sleep

One of the main obstructions to initial learning is late nights. Children often deprive themselves of sleep all the week and try to catch up at weekends by staying in bed until noon. This is not laziness as is often thought, it is a symptom of a bad week of neglected sleep. Reading practice is vital at home but it often gets left until the last thing. It is tempting to say, 'Oh well, leave it until tomorrow.' The trouble is that the same thing happens then. The child is then learning that it is not important.

Rules of Thumb

Reading practice is vital every day but the trouble is in remembering to do it. One way is to lay a reading book on the pupil's pillow so that it has to be picked up before sleeping. Once it is picked up one or two pages should be read. The time taken may be merely a minute or two but it is regularity that matters. Of course more may be read but not so that the next night can be missed. If the bed is rarely made there may be a problem but often the pupil will remember to put the book back on his pillow when he gets up.

Another idea is how to find out if a book is of the right difficulty for a pupil. Take the book and turn to any page and ask the pupil to read it. There should be four 'hard words' on the page. If there are more the pupil may be pushed over his frustration level and he may say that he does not like the book. If there are less than four hard words on the page the book is too easy for him. This does not mean that he should not read it. He may want to practise his newfound skills. He should not be made to read a book that he thinks is too easy for him even if there are more than four hard words on a page.

Another rule-of-thumb measurement and one a pupil can work out for himself is for the pupil to decipher four hard words on his own every day. If he can do this, his reading age will go up by a year more than his real age. Thus he can agree with himself to advance three years more by reading twelve hard words a day. This is not easy to sustain so it is sensible not to set too high a target. The rules are common sense. Do not ask an adult to confirm a word already known. Do not let an adult tell what the word is if it is wrong. Use a reading book to find the words, not a list or dictionary.

Motivation

The above rules of thumb all help with motivation. Good readers can be encouraged to do better as well as others. Good readers tend to find that they can 'read' so they do not bother to push themselves. Poor readers really have to work twice as hard. Anything that can be done to help them is worth trying. This is where the home can help with encouragement.

There is a lot more to learning to read than just working out the words and finding the meaning. Useful advances can be made with précis writing and finding the right words but the fewest, as budding journalists are told. In addition, there is the art of speed reading where the need is to pick out the essential and the most telling words to register the sense.

Before this more advanced stage, the home can help with more simple initial stages. The following suggestions are some of the ways in which all can help.

Paired reading

One of the best ways of helping a child to learn to read and to improve rapidly is to be with him. There are many ways of helping. One of the best ways is to read with him in various ways. Initially, read at the same time as the pupil. He may only be able to manage a few words. Gradually one might advance to both reading at once. If at any time the pupil wishes to read alone he should do so. It might be advantageous for a pupil to follow a story being read slowly from a tape. It might be useful for an adult to read a page and then for the pupil to read one. In this way he can collect praise for his efforts. The story can move along quite quickly and the sense is more easily followed.

Alternate reading

Alternate reading allows the pupil to have a short rest from reading. One can agree to read alternate pages or, initially, the biggest page, leaving the pupil to read a smaller amount. Progress is seen when the pupil asks to stick to alternate pages, whatever the size.

Certainly the home can be a built-in resource that the school cannot afford to ignore.

Conclusion

Giving general advice to the home lacks conviction unless it is followed up in practice. Adults naturally want to do the best for their children if only they knew what to do. Saying they have no time means that the priority comes a long way down the list of importance.

Some parents do not know nursery rhymes and do not see the use of them. Education concerns a child's whole life, most of which is spent at home. Although only a small time is spent at school, it is a particularly important part, especially for poorer readers where learning to read is concerned. It would seem sensible for schools to do all they can to assist the home in the education of their children. There are many ways in which the school might become involved. To intrude would be wrong but to do nothing, surely, is to fall down on the basic idea of education responsibility. The best a school can do is to offer every assistance possible. Whether help is taken up is another matter. Typical would be the case of pupils who have DTT, some of which can be quite severe. The idea of classroom assistants and special needs teachers is excellent for routine application. Where a reception teacher needs most help is in the diagnosis and prevention of problem areas as well as organising suitable rescues. These days, where many schools manage their own finances, several schools should get together to hire a well qualified reading specialist advisor and teacher in order to prevent reading problems. Such a person should liaise with the home as well as helping the school.

The brief should be simple: merely to cut the numbers of poor readers going to the next school still as poor readers.

IN FINALIS

'Experts'

It has generally been considered that there are no 'experts' with regard to the practical teaching of reading. This idea boosts teachers' confidence and saves the education authority a lot of trouble, for they do not need to send in an 'expert' to help. Even a very accomplished and experienced teacher can be made to seem ineffective by a school that does not co-operate. A great deal depends upon the attitude of the school.

Much depends upon the way the teaching has been organised. If the attitude is 'we have done our best, now let's see what a so-called "expert" can do', and the pupil is handed over to the unfortunate 'expert' on a one-to-one basis, then returned to his class to fit in, if he can, the pupil may appear to make little progress. Equally, if the school has done its best and the pupil has still not improved, it is not much use for the teacher to say, 'He is hopeless at x, he wants more practice at y along these lines.' The teacher may be right but work along these lines has not worked before, why should more of the same be the answer?

It would be better for the 'expert' or the special needs teacher or whoever, if they have any expertise, to make a personal diagnosis and say, from an independent and external view, what is thought and discovered. A discussion with the class teacher or head should follow and a way forward should then be agreed. From then on both the 'expert' and the class teacher should work together.

Success can only then be rated as the class teacher's who has spent more time with the pupil than the 'expert'. The 'expert' has helped. An oar has been put in, a rope thrown. It is the class teacher and the pupil who should have all the honour.

Certainly there are rare occasions when an 'expert' steps in, says something and from then on the pupil suddenly races forward. Quite often under these circumstances, the 'expert' has no idea what triggered this reaction. When this occurred at one school, the deputy head asked if she could sit in during the next session. At the end of the time, she withdrew without a word and a door was heard to slam. She was certain that the secret method had been deliberately withheld. Perhaps the answer is hidden somewhere in this book?

Around the Schools

At one time heads of schools could ask for help for pupils who were not progressing. I would visit the school and meet the pupil and the teacher and find out as much as I could before sitting down with the pupil and making a diagnosis. Some were apprehensive but usually were under eight years old, and they soon settled down and relaxed. I often started with an informal chat asking about pets, brothers and sisters and what they did. Sometimes I found that there was no need to ask if there was anything that was troubling them. With Dawn, for instance, it all came out in a rush. 'Mum says she thinks I'm backwards. I've seen the doctor and another man too.' Now she was seeing me. She quite expected me to say that, yes she was 'backwards' but perhaps I could turn her round. I said, 'Well, let's see.' I opened her simple reading book and asked, 'Can you read this at all?' 'Yes,' she said with some relief, and proceeded to stumble through the words quite well. I stopped her after a few lines and said, 'That's not bad. You could soon be good.' I asked her if she had been reading long. She was then seven and obviously was a little behind the average. Her reading age had been given as six and a half, not much below her chronological age. Her teacher and the head thought that she was not progressing fast enough. I could see that it was probably the mother who was pushing a bit. Indeed, I found that her mother had expected Dawn to read as well as her older sister had done. She thought Dawn might be dyslexic. In actual fact, there seemed little amiss although she may have been immature earlier on. This I explained to her as simply as I could. I said, 'When you were young, a bit of your brain had not grown enough for you to be able to read very well but now it has there is nothing wrong at all. You can now learn to read well. I'll help you anyway.' I noted the look of relief and joy on her face. She was not hiding anything. I had seen, as she read, that she was not too sure about the sound build-up of even some of the simpler words. I wondered if she was familiar with letter names. She looked a little sheepish and said, 'Mummy told me what they are called but Miss May said to call them 'a' and 'e' for egg. It looked as if she knew the letter names but was still a bit unsure of letter sounds. I made a note of this. I gathered that Miss May wanted to concentrate on letter sounds rather than names because the two could cause some muddle, and Dawn seemed to be muddled. I thought it wise to use what knowledge Dawn had.

To begin I asked about an 'e' at the end of a word. 'Oh, that is what Miss May calls a magic "e"'. I explained that all the magic 'e' did was to change the a, e, i, o, or u before it to its name. It is useful to know letter names. They can help. She seemed to understand but was dubious about what Miss May would say, so I said, 'Let this be our little secret.' She smiled.

The bell sounded. It was lunchtime. Dawn stood up happily and skipped to the door. I was picking up my books when I heard Dawn exclaim excitedly, 'Mum, he said there is nothing wrong with me.' I went out and shook hands with Dawn's mother. 'She'll be all right,' I said. 'You have nothing to worry about there.' I was smiling and felt radiant. This is what teaching is all about, I thought.

I saw Dawn three or four more times before the headmaster said could I look at another pupil because Dawn was now progressing so well. I agreed. I had a long chat with Miss May, an elderly lady, very kindly and thoughtful. She mentioned that Dawn seemed to be muddled sometimes by the letter names and their sound. I suggested that she used letter names to augment the sounds as with two vowels together.

Kate

At another school the headmaster explained that he had been taking Kate for some weeks for special tuition for her reading but she appeared to be making almost no progress. I saw Kate the next week; she seemed to be a very quiet, timid girl, not at all like Dawn. She answered questions sensibly but gave me the impression that she did not chat. Keep to business was the message. I guessed from her hesitant reading, she was close to being good. There was just one small area that was causing trouble. She seemed to know all the letter sounds but was hesitant with the sound of two vowels together. She was guessing the word from context quite correctly but with a lot of hesitation as though, if she got it wrong she would be shouted at, which made the hesitation worse. I pointed out that nine times out of ten the sound of the two vowels was the same as the name of the first. Anyway, if she got it wrong nobody would shout at her.

The following week the headmaster said, 'I don't know what you did but Kate is reading like she never had a problem.' I was astonished that such a small incident should have made such a difference. I told the headmaster what I had found and what I had told Kate.

Kevin

Not every pupil was a resounding success. Kevin was a distinct failure. It was due to an unfortunate muddle. I saw Kevin's teacher who was worried about his progress. He was over seven but his reading was not up to his general standard. He had an older brother in another class who, she said, was average. I saw Kevin, a bright lad, who seemed to be getting over some immaturity, mostly in the visual area. He still tended to take a quick look at a letter or word, look away and try to guess. As a result he was often wrong. It seemed that he needed practice with looking more carefully for recognition points. It was no use guessing without any idea of differences between words. As a result I soon laid out my cards for a recognition and differentiation game. It did not take Kevin long to learn the differences between similar letters, even b and d, with the word bed, which intrigued him and tickled his sense of fun. His teacher was careful to continue to draw his attention to some differences in words. She had dropped the initial look/say approach in favour of a phonic one, which Kevin appreciated.

Within a short time of about a month, for I saw most pupils once a week for between twenty minutes and half an hour, Kevin had improved a lot with his reading. Then, to my surprise, the headmaster asked me if I would see Kevin's brother instead, as he could do with pulling up. When I met John I sensed at once the animosity he felt. He read from his book. He had a similar visual-type difficulty to what Kevin had. The trouble was now that Kevin was better than John and it was my fault. I told his teacher and the headmaster who apologised for not foreseeing the trouble. I did not see John again. I knew that he would recover eventually, which he did with his teacher's help. I had been very foolish in not checking more thoroughly. I had been big-headed enough to think that the lad would want to see the games his brother had played and try to play them himself. All I had done was to lower his self-esteem and possibly damage his peer prestige without uttering a word.

Advice and assessments

When I was teaching in a class I never thought very highly of advisers. They were never available when required. One had to wait many months for one even if one bothered to come at all. When one did come the advice seemed unrealistic or too general to be of much use. When one asked questions the impression I had was that the adviser was on guard all the time. I had little time for an adviser. Suddenly I was in the position where the head of a school, outside my general area, might ring and ask me to see a pupil and advise on possible action. I was aware of the possible reaction if it was anything like mine. Nevertheless I went, talked to the head and the teacher and assessed the pupil's problems as well as I could. Sad to say that in some cases it was the school, the attitude to the necessary teaching and the teachers' entrenched ideas that were the main problems but could I say that? I proceeded to assess the pupil's needs in order to learn, wrote them all down and left fairly certain that there would be little change, if any. This was proved at one school, which has been referred to in an earlier chapter. I will tell the tale again with a little more detail.

I had a phone call from a middle school on the far edge of my area asking me to see a boy who was causing some concern. My time was fully booked so I could not take on another pupil at that time but I usually reserved Friday mornings in order to assess and report concerning extra pupils, so I went. The boy was the son of a single mother who had complained that not enough was being done to help her son Tom. She felt that he could be doing much better. I saw the lad and I too thought that he could do much better. He had just come from a small country school. It did not take long to find that he was reacting to a younger age range. He had struggled with his initial maturity but was then over the problems of unco-ordination. He may have developed more slowly than some pupils but had just about caught up in most respects. His confidence and self-esteem had taken a battering but his reading ability was not far behind. I calculated that, with more practice, his letter recognition and word differentiation skills would soon be above average. He needed a certain amount of sympathetic help and some success to boost his confidence.

I made and left a detailed report, explained matters to the head and his teacher and left. I heard nothing more until, suddenly, two years later, I was asked to attend a 'case conference', as it was called, concerning a boy from the same school. The name struck a chord so I looked up my records and, sure enough, it was the same boy I had seen two years before. Attending such a case conference were all professional people who had had dealings with the family. There were doctors, psychologists, psychiatrists, social workers, teachers and the school deputy head. In such meetings the family is not represented, which to me, seemed grossly unfair but that is how the system works.

The meeting started and everyone present gave a report. I was shocked and surprised, never having been to a case conference before. The boy was causing some disruption at school and even his mother was finding him more and more of a handful. The psychiatrist backed by the psychologist, social worker and the education officer, thought he should be removed from his deeply disturbed mother's charge and sent to a strict boarding school. Fortunately I still had my report to give and I was glad that I had had the foresight to do some homework. All the other professionals had visited the boy's home or met his mother. I determined to do the same so I had phoned the mother and made an appointment to see her well before the meeting. When I met her I found a very sensible, concerned woman. She told me that Tom had always wanted to join the army. In order to do so he had to pass a particular exam. The school had said that he had no chance at all. The mother thought otherwise. Her pushy attitude had gained her the title of being highly emotionally disturbed. I said that I would see what I could do. I could not promise anything with a phalanx of powerful professionals having their say.

At the meeting I gave my report saying that I had seen Tom two years previously and left recommendations. I could not very well say that none of them had been carried out but I learnt that the head teacher of that time had left and the present head was only a term old. I put my case that I thought that matters were redeemable and I was now able to fit the boy into my schedule for, possibly, two terms.

Presumably potential cost came into it so the education officer decided that I should have the chance to redeem matters for a while before things were taken further.

The following week I saw Tom's teacher who was very helpful and co-operative. I spent the next few weeks going through many basic elements of letter and word recognition in the form of games. I found that there was little wrong with his capabilities. He needed to take more care before making hurried decisions and guesses but, most of all, he needed his confidence boosting. I tried to help by proving to him that he could do things well and be right, but not to be afraid of making mistakes from which he could learn.

At the end of that term he had come top of his class. His teacher had given him a massive boost of self-esteem. I had seen him once a week for half an hour at a time. The following term I saw Tom occasionally, mostly for him to illustrate something new that he had learnt. At the end of that term he had held his top position so I did not see him again.

Several years later I received a letter from Tom's mother thanking me for helping him and telling me that Tom had passed the critical army exam and was very happy. I felt fortunate that I had been there in time to save a boy's life from being ruined.

Daphne & Derek

Another time I was asked to see Daphne at a large school out of my area. It took me less than two minutes, when I heard her trying to read, to find that she did not recognise many letters either by sight or sound. She had done extremely well to get as far as she had by the look/say and context method. When she came to an unknown word she had no idea how to glean a clue about it. It shocked me to find a girl aged twelve, who must have had seven years of teachers and not one of them had noticed that she did not know the letters and, if they did, had never bothered to help her learn them.

When I told the headmaster he turned to the girl and said, 'Daphne, go home and learn your letters, girl.' I thought that was a stupid thing to say. She obviously had no idea how to learn her letters.

If I was shocked by Daphne's case I was stunned by a boy, Derek, at another large school, again well outside my area. I was kept waiting by the boy's teacher. When I went to look for him I discovered him behind a screen sniffing glue. I said nothing to him about this. I was disgusted. Derek, I found, had been taught exclusively, by the look/say method and there he was stuck. He knew letter names but not their sounds and had no idea of how to begin gaining clues by building letter sounds. Nobody had picked this up or showed him any other ways of learning. Now he was fourteen.

What shocked me even more was that when I left my report with the headmaster he was mystified and rang the chief education officer saying that he did not understand my report. He did not know of a phonic approach.

The chief education officer replied by getting the school a specialist reading teacher. My visit did some good after all.

Donald

Donald was a lively boy at a first school nearby. I was asked to try to help with a boy who was disruptive and not learning. I knew the headmaster and had played golf with him so we talked 'shop' about Donald a bit. I found Donald to be a willing, lively chap who wanted to talk. I saw him one-to-one as usual for half an hour a week. He was never awkward and quite willing to work. It was difficult to believe the lurid tales I had been told about him. Then one day I arrived a little early. The headmaster greeted me like a saviour. 'I'm so glad you've come now. You hear that noise?' Indeed I could. A toilet door was being banged and kicked repeatedly. The headmaster went and called Donald to say that I had arrived for him. The noise stopped at once and a shamed-faced Donald appeared. 'Was that you making that noise?' I asked. Donald nodded. 'What was it all about?' I asked. He looked sheepish but said quite honestly, 'I was bored. There is never anything to do.' Donald worked away well at the word games and exercises and some reading very well. His frustration and annoyance was forgotten. It seemed that his teacher did not know how to handle him and the headmaster was no better, what could I do?

At that time I knew the local education officer so I had a word with him. He had an immediate solution. He asked me if I thought the boy would do better at another school. I agreed. Donald was moved to another school and all the trouble ended. This was a happy ending to an unusual case.

Ted

For Ted it was a different matter. He was not a clever boy, having an average intelligence, but he had some trouble with his hand/eye co-ordination. He had some dyslexic-type difficulties, which were to do with his late maturation in his visual and auditory areas. This was causing him to be untidy with his writing. He was slow with the differentiation of some letters and words. He was one who worked hard but had little to show for it, making it appear that he was well below average in intelligence. The school was a tiny one-teacher school in an expanding village. It probably does not exist any more now. The headmaster was a kindly, old-fashioned disciplinarian due to retire in three years when he asked me to help with Ted who, he was afraid, would leave with a very low standard. I went through my appropriate assessments to confirm and clarify my initial guesswork. He was rather a slow learner but was a hard worker. This compensated for many of his lesser abilities. As I suspected, he knew most of his letters by name and sound but had to think hard on occasions, which made him slow and hesitant. He could be flustered if pushed, which made things worse. He reversed and muddled the usual similar letters and was hesitant and unsure of some letter sounds. In particular two vowels together confused him sometimes. This gave me a good start with reading and writing as well as helping him gain more confidence in his ability to succeed. He would never be a fast worker but he could be careful, though, and accurate. Most of the trouble in attaining this seemed to be with his teacher whose consistent attitude was to try to push Ted along with some impatience and intolerance. He did not seem to understand that Ted's untidiness was due to his poor hand/eye co-ordination, which was not deliberate laziness or carelessness.

I found this one week, when I helped Ted with writing a story, which he did very well. Even the writing was better than usual because he was more relaxed. He really tried with that story. He was sure his headmaster would be pleased. When I came the following week I asked him how his story had been accepted. To my surprise, his eyes filled with tears. He choked out the words, 'He didn't even look at it. He tore it up because it wasn't neat enough.'

I always stayed an extra five minutes to have a word with the teacher. It took me eleven months of those five minutes to get across what Ted needed. Suddenly, after that, Ted began to change. His confidence grew. He even walked more upright and I saw the two of them working together and both were smiling. I knew Ted would be okay after that. The following year the headmaster retired and I regretted his going.

John

I was asked to go to another small two-teacher first school to assess a boy whose trouble was very similar to Ted's. The headmistress was elderly and due to retire at the end of that year. John's teacher was another lady who then became headmistress. She was very good with the majority of the pupils but had no time for John. John worked all the time but very slowly. His object seemed to be to manage with as little trouble as possible. The teacher 'contained' him. Most of the lessons sailed over John's head. Much of the time he would busy himself finishing an exercise or some other work.

I always spoke to the teacher about John and his needs but I knew that nothing would change. I did what I could with one half hour a week but, with no follow-up or backing from his teacher, I felt that John would be below his potential when he went to his secondary school. I always felt sorry that I could not have done more for John. I hadn't failed but I hadn't won. It made me realise how important a pupil's teacher at his school really was. If I had been the best expert in the world, without his class teacher's backing I felt I would still have been nearly useless.

Jake

How different it was at another small two-teacher first school. The headmistress rang one day asking if I would assess the needs of a boy. I went and found two very intelligent, thoughtful ladies. The boy was a local farmer's son whose parents were influential people in the area. Jake was by no means lacking in intelligence but, in spite of all best efforts, was not progressing well. I did my standard assessment test concerning letters and words and found that he was weak both visually and in auditory appreciation. He had been slow to begin talking when a baby and slow with his development, but now his sluggishness appeared to be clearing. He was taking much more interest in many areas which indicated that, with concentration and hard work, he would do quite well although he may not attain to academic brilliance unless he became very interested in a particular thing. He was not dyslexic but showed some dyslexic-type tendencies, which could be overcome to a great extent. I felt that it would take some time but, with good teaching and his will to learn, he could do well.

I reported my findings and was pleased to hear that they agreed with all I said. My assessment coincided with their own judgements. The headmistress told me that she had some trepidation in asking me to see Jake because, some years before, they had asked for help. Along had come a person understood to be an expert but they had experienced what they called a disaster. She was pleased that I was different. I worked with the two ladies for about a year when I felt that there was little else that I could add to their knowledge and experience with Jake.

Joe

I called at one large first school, which was what I would term a traditional one. It was an old-fashioned building and the teachers were all similar. They kept good discipline but the difference was that it was excellent when a teacher was there but one could tell at once if there was no teacher in the room. The pupils were noisy and unruly. As soon as a teacher arrived all was quiet.

I called there to help with a boy who was deemed to be working below his potential. I found that he was a sensitive lad and quite intelligent. I was not keen on his teacher who, it seemed to me, was not sympathetic towards Joe. He had no empathy, I thought. This was confirmed on my second visit. I called at the classroom and asked for Joe. The teacher was asking questions round the class. Immediately he turned to Joe. He could not answer. There was a snigger round the class. The teacher smiled and said, 'Go on, Joe, to your extra reading.' Joe came out in a black mood and I could not blame him. Fortunately he soon settled down and we had a good session.

The trouble was that Joe was going back to a class and situation in which he would learn little. How could I tell his teacher that his attitude was not conducive to this boy learning? I took care not to try to help that teacher. I was probably wrong but I was unable to 'pull rank' on him as I was just another teacher. He was innocently trying to illustrate to me just how 'thick' Joe was. To me it was an illustration of very poor teaching practice.

Fortunately for Joe it was the end of the year and he was

in another class the following year where he really began to learn.

It was at the same school but another class where there was a shy, sensitive boy. His teacher seemed a quiet, kindly lady. When Keith came he seemed upset but I could not guess why. He said that he felt all right. He accomplished the assessment games and exercises very well. I found that he was only a little behind, typical of someone who had missed a crucial stage of learning to read and was struggling to work out how to make sense of the words more quickly. I thought that he would soon pick up. His teacher agreed with my assessment and said that she was giving him plenty of practice. The next visit again he looked on the verge of tears. I asked him if it upset him to come out to me. I had hit the nail on the head. The tears really flowed. 'Look,' I said, 'you have come here because you are doing well. Your teacher thinks that with a bit of extra help you could be very good. You know that you are not the worst reader in the class, don't you?' He nodded. 'I bet you know several who are not as good as you.' He nodded again. 'Let's start, then, you'll see.'

We started with vowel names and how they can be used to find their sound in words. This was obviously new to him and he caught the idea at once. It only took a term for him to catch up. I wondered where he had got the idea that my help was some sort of disgrace, but he was not the only one to have this idea.

I had a phone call one day from a headteacher in a tiny one-teacher first school. She was concerned about one of her boys. I went and had a long chat. I saw the boy fleetingly and made an appointment to see him next week. A few days before my pending visit she rang again. She said that she had changed her mind. She did not think it was fair on the boy to subject him to the trauma of seeing me for help. What had I done? What had I said wrong? She seemed such a pleasant, caring woman. Had I not 'sold' myself well enough? My approach had worked with many. Some, in fact, had become firm friends for many years. Was it that I was a man and the boy had never seen such a terrifying man teacher before? This seemed to be somewhere near the favourite thought. I remembered that many years before, when I first came out of college, being given the top class of an infant school. The headmistress explained that to have me take the class would give these young children some experience of having a man teacher, which they could expect to have some time in their next school. I must admit that never afterwards did I ever have a class full of children whose behaviour was so good.

One of my favourite schools was a large new first school where the headmaster became a good friend. The school was a complete contrast to the other large school. Here it was impossible to tell if the teacher was in the classroom or not. The atmosphere was exactly the same. There was a quiet buzz of a pupil or two quietly discussing a point of work with a neighbour while at other tables the teacher might be sitting helping other children. Everyone had something to do and they were all getting on with it. Occasionally the teacher might go to another room to fetch something while things went on just the same. Once I noticed a boy playing about but immediately three others told him to get on and not to disturb them. It worked.

I had a very good relationship with one reception teacher who, during our chats, picked up all the elements needed to assess and diagnose any possible needs of pupils. Any pupil she was unsure about she referred to me.

Finally the headmaster thought that it would be a good idea for me to see and assess every first-year pupil. Unfortunately one boy was the son of an educational psychologist. She made it plain to the headmaster that she thought that it was a waste of time to test her son. The headmaster was quite upset. I said that I thought it was really none of her business how he ran his school. She should stick to psychological matters. I completed all the assessments that week so there was no more to say.

Joan

Talking about psychology made me think of an occasion when I was asked to diagnose the needs of Joan, the daughter of a teacher at another school. The headmaster was quite a pompous little man who was also the secretary of our golf club. He asked me to see Joan who seemed unable to progress although she had been doing quite well. When I saw her she was unable to do simple calculations although she knew her tables well. This gave me an immediate clue, which I followed up. I was certain that Joan was emotionally disturbed. The headmaster disagreed. He showed me her work. She recited a poem. In the end he agreed to ask an educational psychologist to see her. A very pleasant young lady came the next week. She said that this would be her last call before being married. Within a very short time she said that Joan was a classic case of emotional disturbance.

The headmaster never forgave me. He got his own back on me later by losing all details of two cups I won at golf, so no name was put on the board that year. Mine could be a touchy, dangerous job, it seemed!

I saw many hundreds of pupils over the decade or so I was there. My initial brief was to prevent non-readers clogging up the secondary schools. Initially the local school had two large classes of very poor and non-readers. After several years there were none. During that time I worked for many hours on simplifying a means of assessing and diagnosing what was preventing perfectly capable pupils from learning to read. When I first started I wanted to know if there was a correlation between a reluctance to learn to read and very poor hand/eye co-ordination. I devised a list and took it to a school but the teacher insisted that all her pupils could do all the tasks perfectly well. I knew that it could not be so but I was not going to progress much in that way.

Teachers were very protective of their pupils. Some teachers insisted that all their pupils could read adequately but when they arrived at their next school somehow all their ability had evaporated. I worked so that all the first-school teachers knew what standard was acceptable and to ask for help when a pupil did not reach that standard. Over the years it seemed to work. However, over the 'grapevine' I heard that my area had then become a 'middle class' area, where I presume, there never are any pupils who ever experience difficulty in learning to read. If they do the teachers are then so good that they are able to sort out any problems with no trouble. Strange how the secondary schools have large classes of poor readers and that there are continual reports of a twenty per cent or more of inadequate readers leaving schools all over the country.